KING LOG

By the same author

FOR THE UNFALLEN
MERCIAN HYMNS
TENEBRAE

GEOFFREY HILL

King Log

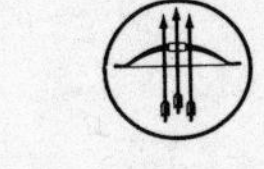

ANDRE DEUTSCH

FIRST PUBLISHED AUGUST 1968 BY
ANDRE DEUTSCH LIMITED
105 GREAT RUSSELL STREET
LONDON WC1

SECOND IMPRESSION SEPTEMBER 1970
THIRD IMPRESSION FEBRUARY 1976
FOURTH IMPRESSION APRIL 1981

PRINTED IN GREAT BRITAIN BY
BILLING & SONS LTD
GUILDFORD, LONDON AND WORCESTER
ISBN 0 233 96289 1

To
KENNETH CURTIS

ACKNOWLEDGMENTS

Acknowledgments and thanks are due to the E. C. Gregory Trust and to the following publications and programmes: *Agenda; The Listener; Living Arts; New Statesman; Of Books and Humankind; The Paris Review; Poetry Now* (B.B.C. Third Programme); *Stand; The Times Literary Supplement;* X: *A Quarterly Review.*

Ten of the poems printed here were first collected in the pamphlet *Preghiere* (Northern House, 1964). A selection included in *Penguin Modern Poets 8* (1966) consisted of poems from my first book and from the pamphlet, together with a few uncollected pieces which now appear in *King Log.*

CONTENTS

From moral virtue let us pass on to matter of power and commandment...

ADVANCEMENT OF LEARNING

KING LOG

OVID IN THE THIRD REICH

non peccat, quaecumque potest peccasse negare,
solaque famosam culpa professa facit.
(Amores, III, xiv)

I love my work and my children. God
Is distant, difficult. Things happen.
Too near the ancient troughs of blood
Innocence is no earthly weapon.

I have learned one thing: not to look down
So much upon the damned. They, in their sphere,
Harmonize strangely with the divine
Love. I, in mine, celebrate the love-choir.

ANNUNCIATIONS

I

The Word has been abroad, is back, with a tanned look
From its subsistence in the stiffening-mire.
Cleansing has become killing, the reward
Touchable, overt, clean to the touch.
Now at a distance from the steam of beasts,
The loathly neckings and fat shook spawn
(Each specimen-jar fed with delicate spawn)
The searchers with the curers sit at meat
And are satisfied. Such precious things put down
And the flesh eased through turbulence the soul
Purples itself; each eye squats full and mild
While all who attend to fiddle or to harp
For betterment, flavour their decent mouths
With gobbets of the sweetest sacrifice.

2

O Love, subject of the mere diurnal grind,
Forever being pledged to be redeemed,
Expose yourself for charity; be assured
The body is but husk and excrement.
Enter these deaths according to the law,
O visited women, possessed sons! Foreign lusts
Infringe our restraints; the changeable
Soldiery have their goings-out and comings-in
Dying in abundance. Choicest beasts
Suffuse the gutters with their colourful blood.
Our God scatters corruption. Priests, martyrs,
Parade to this imperious theme: 'O Love,
You know what pains succeed; be vigilant; strive
To recognize the damned among your friends.'

LOCUST SONGS

To Allan Seager

THE EMBLEM

So with sweet oaths converting the salt earth
To yield, our fathers verged on Paradise:
Each to his own portion of Paradise,
Stung by the innocent venoms of the earth.

GOOD HUSBANDRY

Out of the foliage of sensual pride
Those teeming apples! Summer burned well
The dramatic flesh; made work for pride
Forking into the tender mouths of Hell

Heaped windfalls, pulp for the Gadarene
Squealers. This must be our reward:
To smell God writhing over the rich scene.
Gluttons for wrath, we stomach our reward.

SHILOH CHURCH, 1862: TWENTY-THREE THOUSAND

O stamping-ground of the shod Word! So hard
On the heels of the damned red-man we came,
Geneva's tribe, outlandish and abhorred –
Bland vistas milky with Jehovah's calm –

Who fell to feasting Nature, the glare
Of buzzards circling; cried to the grim sun
'Jehovah punish us!'; who went too far;
In deserts dropped the odd white turds of bone;

Whose passion was to find out God in this
His natural filth, voyeur of sacrifice, a slow
Bloody unearthing of the God-in-us.
But with what blood, and to what end, Shiloh?

I HAD HOPE WHEN VIOLENCE WAS CEAS'T

Dawnlight freezes against the east-wire.
The guards cough 'raus! 'raus! We flinch and grin,
Our flesh oozing towards its last outrage.
That which is taken from me is not mine.

SEPTEMBER SONG

born 19.6.32 – deported 24.9.42

Undesirable you may have been, untouchable
you were not. Not forgotten
or passed over at the proper time.

As estimated, you died. Things marched,
sufficient, to that end.
Just so much Zyklon and leather, patented
terror, so many routine cries.

(I have made
an elegy for myself it
is true)

September fattens on vines. Roses
flake from the wall. The smoke
of harmless fires drifts to my eyes.

This is plenty. This is more than enough.

AN ORDER OF SERVICE

He was the surveyor of his own ice-world,
Meticulous at the chosen extreme,
Though what he surveyed may have been nothing.

Let a man sacrifice himself, concede
His mortality and have done with it;
There is no end to that sublime appeal.

In such a light dismiss the unappealing
Blank of his gaze, hopelessly vigilant,
Dazzled by renunciation's glare.

THE HUMANIST

The *Venice* portrait: he
Broods, the achieved guest
Tired and word-perfect
At the Muses' table.

Virtue is virtù. These
Lips debate and praise –
Some rich aphorism;
A delicate white meat.

The commonplace hands once
Thick with Plato's blood
(Tasteless! tasteless!) are laid
Dryly against the robes.

FUNERAL MUSIC

William de la Pole, Duke of Suffolk: beheaded 1450
John Tiptoft, Earl of Worcester: beheaded 1470
Anthony Woodville, Earl Rivers: beheaded 1483

I

Processionals in the exemplary cave,
Benediction of shadows. Pomfret. London.
The voice fragrant with mannered humility,
With an equable contempt for this World,
'In honorem Trinitatis'. Crash. The head
Struck down into a meaty conduit of blood.
So these dispose themselves to receive each
Pentecostal blow from axe or seraph,
Spattering block-straw with mortal residue.
Psalteries whine through the empyrean. Fire
Flares in the pit, ghosting upon stone
Creatures of such rampant state, vacuous
Ceremony of possession, restless
Habitation, no man's dwelling-place.

2

For whom do we scrape our tribute of pain –
For none but the ritual king? We meditate
A rueful mystery; we are dying
To satisfy fat Caritas, those
Wiped jaws of stone. (Suppose all reconciled
By silent music; imagine the future
Flashed back at us, like steel against sun,
Ultimate recompense.) Recall the cold
Of Towton on Palm Sunday before dawn,
Wakefield, Tewkesbury: fastidious trumpets
Shrilling into the ruck; some trampled
Acres, parched, sodden or blanched by sleet,
Stuck with strange-postured dead. Recall the wind's
Flurrying, darkness over the human mire.

3

They bespoke doomsday and they meant it by
God, their curved metal rimming the low ridge.
But few appearances are like this. Once
Every five hundred years a comet's
Over-riding stillness might reveal men
In such array, livid and featureless,
With England crouched beastwise beneath it all.
'Oh, that old northern business . . .' A field
After battle utters its own sound
Which is like nothing on earth, but is earth.
Blindly the questing snail, vulnerable
Mole emerge, blindly we lie down, blindly
Among carnage the most delicate souls
Tup in their marriage-blood, gasping 'Jesus'.

4

Let mind be more precious than soul; it will not
Endure. Soul grasps its price, begs its own peace,
Settles with tears and sweat, is possibly
Indestructible. That I can believe.
Though I would scorn the mere instinct of faith,
Expediency of assent, if I dared,
What I dare not is a waste history
Or void rule. Averroes, old heathen,
If only you had been right, if Intellect
Itself were absolute law, sufficient grace,
Our lives could be a myth of captivity
Which we might enter: an unpeopled region
Of ever new-fallen snow, a palace blazing
With perpetual silence as with torches.

5

As with torches we go, at wild Christmas,
When we revel in our atonement
Through thirty feasts of unction and slaughter,
What is that but the soul's winter sleep?
So many things rest under consummate
Justice as though trumpets purified law,
Spikenard were the real essence of remorse.
The sky gathers up darkness. When we chant
'Ora, ora pro nobis' it is not
Seraphs who descend to pity but ourselves.
Those righteously-accused those vengeful
Racked on articulate looms indulge us
With lingering shows of pain, a flagrant
Tenderness of the damned for their own flesh:

6

My little son, when you could command marvels
Without mercy, outstare the wearisome
Dragon of sleep, I rejoiced above all –
A stranger well-received in your kingdom.
On those pristine fields I saw humankind
As it was named by the Father; fabulous
Beasts rearing in stillness to be blessed.
The world's real cries reached there, turbulence
From remote storms, rumour of solitudes,
A composed mystery. And so it ends.
Some parch for what they were; others are made
Blind to all but one vision, their necessity
To be reconciled. I believe in my
Abandonment, since it is what I have.

7

'Prowess, vanity, mutual regard,
It seemed I stared at them, they at me.
That was the gorgon's true and mortal gaze:
Averted conscience turned against itself.'
A hawk and a hawk-shadow. 'At noon,
As the armies met, each mirrored the other;
Neither was outshone. So they flashed and vanished
And all that survived them was the stark ground
Of this pain. I made no sound, but once
I stiffened as though a remote cry
Had heralded my name. It was nothing . . .'
Reddish ice tinged the reeds; dislodged, a few
Feathers drifted across; carrion birds
Strutted upon the armour of the dead.

8

Not as we are but as we must appear,
Contractual ghosts of pity; not as we
Desire life but as they would have us live,
Set apart in timeless colloquy:
So it is required; so we bear witness,
Despite ourselves, to what is beyond us,
Each distant sphere of harmony forever
Poised, unanswerable. If it is without
Consequence when we vaunt and suffer, or
If it is not, all echoes are the same
In such eternity. Then tell me, love,
How that should comfort us – or anyone
Dragged half-unnerved out of this worldly place,
Crying to the end 'I have not finished'.

FOUR POEMS REGARDING THE ENDURANCE OF POETS

MEN ARE A MOCKERY OF ANGELS

i.m. Tommaso Campanella, priest and poet

Some days a shadow through
The high window shares my
Prison. I watch a slug
Scale the glinting pit-side
Of its own slime. The cries
As they come are mine; then
God's: my justice, wounds, love,
Derisive light, bread, filth.

To lie here in my strange
Flesh while glutted Torment
Sleeps, stained with its prompt food,
Is a joy past all care
Of the world, for a time.
But we are commanded
To rise, when, in silence,
I would compose my voice.

A PRAYER TO THE SUN

i.m. Miguel Hernandez

i

Darkness
above all things
the Sun
makes
rise

ii

Vultures
salute their meat
at noon
(Hell is
silent)

iii

Blind Sun
our ravager
bless us
so that
we sleep.

'DOMAINE PUBLIC'

i.m. Robert Desnos, died Terezin Camp, 1945

For reading I can recommend
  the Fathers. How they
cultivate the corrupting flesh:

toothsome contemplation: cleanly
  maggots churning spleen
to milk. For exercise, prolonged

suppression of much improper
  speech from proper tombs.
If the ground opens, should men's mouths

open also? 'I am nothing
  if not saved now!' or
'Christ, what a pantomime!' The days

of the week are seven pits. Look,
  Seigneur, again we
resurrect and the judges come.

A Valediction to Osip Mandelshtam

Difficult friend, I would have preferred
You to them. The dead keep their sealed lives
And again I am too late. Too late
The salutes, dust-clouds and brazen cries.

Images rear from desolation
Look . . . ruins upon a plain . . .
A few men glare at their hands; others
Grovel for food in the roadside field.

Tragedy has all under regard.
It will not touch us but it is there –
Flawless, insatiate – hard summer sky
Feasting on this, reaching its own end.

THE IMAGINATIVE LIFE

Evasive souls, of whom the wise lose track,
Die in each night, who, with their day-tongues, sift
The waking-taste of manna or of blood:

The raw magi, part-barbarians,
Entranced by demons and desert frost,
By the irregular visions of a god,

Suffragans of the true seraphs. Lust
Writhes, is dumb savage and in their way
As a virulence natural to the earth.

Renewed glories batten on the poor bones;
Gargantuan mercies whetted by a scent
Of mortal sweat: as though the sleeping flesh

Adored by Furies, stirred, yawned, were driven
In mid-terror to purging and delight.
As though the dead had *Finis* on their brows.

THE ASSISI FRAGMENTS

To G. Wilson Knight

I

Lion and lioness, the mild
Inflammable beasts,
At their precise peril kept
Distance and repose –
And there the serpent
Innocently shone its head.

2

So the hawk had its pursuit. So Death
Opened its childish eyes. So the angels
Overcame Adam: he was defiled
By balm. Creator, and creature made
Of unnatural earth, he howled
To the raven *find me;* to the wolf
Eat, my brother; and to the fire *I am clean.*

HISTORY AS POETRY

Poetry as salutation; taste
Of Pentecost's ashen feast. Blue wounds.
The tongue's atrocities. Poetry
Unearths from among the speechless dead

Lazarus mystified, common man
Of death. The lily rears its gouged face
From the provided loam. Fortunate
Auguries; whirrings; tarred golden dung:

'A resurgence' as they say. The old
Laurels wagging with the new: Selah!
Thus laudable the trodden bone thus
Unanswerable the knack of tongues.

SOLILOQUIES

THE STONE MAN

To Charles Causley

Recall, now, the omens of childhood:
The nettle-clump and rank elder-tree;
The stones waiting in the mason's yard:

Half-recognized kingdom of the dead:
A deeper landscape lit by distant
Flashings from their journey. At nightfall

My father scuffed clay into the house.
He set his boots on the bleak iron
Of the hearth; ate, drank, unbuckled, slept.

I leaned to the lamp; the pallid moths
Clipped its glass, made an autumnal sound.
Words clawed my mind as though they had smelt

Revelation's flesh . . . So, with an ease
That is dreadful, I summon all back.
The sun bellows over its parched swarms.

OLD POET WITH DISTANT ADMIRERS

What I lost was not a part of this.
The dark-blistered foxgloves, wet berries
Glinting from shadow, small ferns and stones,

Seem fragments, in the observing mind,
Of its ritual power. Old age
Singles them out as though by first-light,

As though a still-life, preserving some
Portion of the soul's feast, went with me
Everywhere, to be hung in strange rooms,

Loneliness being what it is. If
I knew the exact coin for tribute,
Defeat might be bought, processional

Silence gesture its tokens of earth
At my mouth: as in the great death-songs
Of Propertius (although he died young).

COWAN BRIDGE

At the site of 'Lowood School'

A lost storm in this temperate place;
The silent direction;
Some ash-trees and foam-patched
Alders at the beck.

All the seasons absorbed
As by a child, safe from rain,
Crouched in the dank
Stench of an elder-bush.

So much that was not justice,
So much that is;
The vulnerable pieties
Not willingly let die;
By chance unmolested
The modesty of her rage.

FANTASIA ON 'HORBURY'

J.B.D. 1859

Dry walls, and nettles battered by the dust,
Odours from gathered water, muddled storm-clouds
Disastrous over the manufactured West Riding.

Mind – a fritter of excrement; step
Aside, step aside, sir! Ah, but a priest
In his prime watches where he goes. He goes

To tender his confession. Forgiveness
Journeys towards him like a brisk traveller
On the same road. Is this Horbury?

Yes: and he will perpetuate this refuge.
Yes: and he will weaken, scribbling, at the end,
Of unspeakable desolation. Really? Good Lord!

Consider him thus animated,
That outworn piety and those plush tunes
Restored for the sake of a paradox

And the too-fashionable North. Or, again,
Consider him catspawed by an indolent poem,
This place not of his choosing, this menace

From concave stormlight a freak suggestion . . .
These heads of nettles lopped into the dust . . .

THREE BAROQUE MEDITATIONS

I

Do words make up the majesty
Of man, and his justice
Between the stones and the void?

How they watch us, the demons
Plugging their dumb wounds! When
Exorcized they shrivel yet thrive.

An owl plunges to its tryst
With a field-mouse in the sharp night.
My fire squeals and lies still.

Minerva, receive this hard
Praise: I speak well of Death;
I confess to the priest in me;

I am shadowed by the wise bird
Of necessity, the lithe
Paradigm Sleep-and-Kill.

2

Anguish bloated by the replete scream.
Flesh of abnegation: the poem
Moves grudgingly to its extreme form,

Vulnerable, to the lamp's fierce head
Of well-trimmed light. In darkness outside,
Foxes and rain-sleeked stones and the dead –

Aliens of such a theme – endure
Until I could cry 'Death! Death!' as though
To exacerbate that suave power;

But refrain. For I am circumspect,
Lifting the spicy lid of my tact
To sniff at the myrrh. It is perfect

In its impalpable bitterness,
Scent of a further country where worse
Furies promenade and bask their claws.

3 THE DEAD BRIDE

So white I was, he would have me cry
  'Unclean!' murderously
To heal me with far-fetched blood.

I writhed to conceive of him.
I clawed to becalm him.
Some nights, I witnessed his face in sleep

And dreamed of my father's
House. (By day he professed languages –
  Disciplines of languages) –

By day I cleansed my pink tongue
From its nightly prowl, its vixen-skill,
  His sacramental mouth

  That justified my flesh
And moved well among women
In nuances and imperatives.

This was the poet of a people's
  Love. I hated him. He weeps,
Solemnizing his loss.

THE SONGBOOK
OF
SEBASTIAN ARRURRUZ

Sebastian Arrurruz: 1868–1922

I

Ten years without you. For so it happens.
Days make their steady progress, a routine
That is merciful and attracts nobody.

Already, like a disciplined scholar,
I piece fragments together, past conjecture
Establishing true sequences of pain;

For so it is proper to find value
In a bleak skill, as in the thing restored:
The long-lost words of choice and valediction.

COPLAS

i

'One cannot lose what one has not possessed'.
So much for that abrasive gem.
I can lose what I want. I want you.

ii

Oh my dear one, I shall grieve for you
For the rest of my life with slightly
Varying cadence, oh my dear one.

iii

Half-mocking the half-truth, I note
'The wild brevity of sensual love'.
I am shaken, even by that.

iv

It is to him I write, it is to her
I speak in contained silence. Will they be touched
By the unfamiliar passion between them?

3

What other men do with other women
Is for me neither orgy nor sacrament
Nor a language of foreign candour

But is mere occasion or chance distance
Out of which you might move and speak my name
As I speak yours, bargaining with sleep's

Miscellaneous gods for as much
As I can have: an alien landscape,
The dream where you are always to be found.

4

A workable fancy. Old petulant
Sorrow comes back to us, metamorphosed
And semi-precious. Fortuitous amber.
As though this recompensed our deprivation.
See how each fragment kindles as we turn it,
At the end, into the light of appraisal.

5

Love, oh my love, it will come
Sure enough! A storm
Broods over the dry earth all day.
At night the shutters throb in its downpour.

The metaphor holds; is a snug house.
You are outside, lost somewhere. I find myself
Devouring verses of stranger passion
And exile. The exact words

Are fed into my blank hunger for you.

POSTURES

I imagine, as I imagine us
Each time more stylized more lovingly
Detailed, that I am not myself
But someone I might have been: sexless,
Indulgent about art, relishing
Let us say the well-schooled
Postures of *St Anthony* or *St Jerome*,
Those peaceful hermaphrodite dreams
Through which the excess of memory
Pursues its own abstinence.

FROM THE LATIN

There would have been things to say, quietness
That could feed on our lust, refreshed
Trivia, the occurrences of the day;
And at night my tongue in your furrow.

Without you I am mocked by courtesies
And chat, where satisfied women push
Dutifully toward some unneeded guest
Desirable features of conversation.

[*1922*]

A LETTER FROM ARMENIA

So, remotely, in your part of the world:
the ripe glandular blooms, and cypresses
shivering with heat (which we have borne
also, in our proper ways) I turn my mind
towards delicate pillage, the provenance
of shards glazed and unglazed, the three
kinds of surviving grain. I hesitate amid
circumstantial disasters. I gaze at the
authentic dead.

A SONG FROM ARMENIA

Roughly-silvered leaves that are the snow
On Ararat seen through those leaves.
The sun lays down a foliage of shade.

A drinking-fountain pulses its head
Two or three inches from the troughed stone.
An old woman sucks there, gripping the rim.

Why do I have to relive, even now,
Your mouth, and your hand running over me
Deft as a lizard, like a sinew of water?

TO HIS WIFE

You ventured occasionally –
As though this were another's house –
Not intimate but an acquaintance
Flaunting her modest claim; like one
Idly commiserated by new-mated
Lovers rampant in proper delight
When all their guests have gone.

[*1921*]

11

Scarcely speaking: it becomes as a
Coolness between neighbours. Often
There is this orgy of sleep. I wake
To caress propriety with odd words
And enjoy abstinence in a vocation
Of now-almost-meaningless despair.

POSTSCRIPT
KING STORK

FUNERAL MUSIC
an essay

In this sequence I was attempting a florid grim music broken by grunts and shrieks. Ian Nairn's description of Eltham Palace as 'a perfect example of the ornate heartlessness of much mid-fifteenth-century architecture, especially court architecture'[1] is pertinent, though I did not read Nairn until after the sequence had been completed. The Great Hall was made for Edward IV. *Funeral Music* could be called a commination and an alleluia for the period popularly but inexactly known as the Wars of the Roses. It bears an oblique dedication. In the case of Suffolk the word 'beheaded' is a retrospective aggrandisement; he was in fact butchered across the gunwale of a skiff. Tiptoft enjoyed a degree of ritual, commanding that he should be decapitated in three strokes 'in honour of the Trinity'. This was a nice compounding of orthodox humility and unorthodox arrogance. Did Tiptoft see himself as Everyman's emblem or as the unique figure preserved in the tableau of his own death? As historic characters Suffolk, Worcester and Rivers haunt the mind vulnerable alike to admiration and scepticism. Was Suffolk – the friend of the captive poet Charles d'Orleans and an advocate of peace with France – a visionary or a racketeer? The Woodville clan invites irritated dismissal: pushful, time-serving, it was really not its business to produce a man like Earl Rivers, who was something of a religious mystic and whose translation, *The Dictes and Sayings of the Philosophers*, was the first book printed in England by Caxton. Suffolk and Rivers were poets, though quite tame. Tiptoft, patron of humanist scholars, was known as the Butcher of England because of his pleasure in varying the accepted postures of judicial death.

Admittedly, the sequence avoids shaping these characters and events into any overt narrative or dramatic structure. The whole inference, though, has value if it gives a key to the ornate and heartless music punctuated by mutterings, blasphemies and cries for help.

There is a distant fury of battle. Without attempting factual detail, I had in mind the Battle of Towton, fought on Palm Sunday, 1461. It is now customary to play down the violence of the Wars of the Roses and to present them as dynastic skirmishes fatal, perhaps, to the old aristocracy but generally of small concern to the common people and without much effect on the economic routines of the kingdom. Statistically, this may be arguable; imaginatively, the Battle of Towton itself commands one's belated witness. In the accounts of the contemporary chroniclers it was a holocaust. Some scholars have suggested that the claims were exaggerated, although the military historian, Colonel A. H. Burne, argues convincingly for the reasonableness of the early estimates. He reckons that over twenty-six thousand men died at Towton and remarks that 'the scene must have beggared description and its very horror probably deterred the survivors from passing on stories of the fight'.[2] Even so, one finds the chronicler of Croyland Abbey writing that the blood of the slain lay caked with the snow which covered the ground and that, when the snow melted, the blood flowed along the furrows and ditches for a distance of two or three miles.[3]

[1] Ian Nairn, *Nairn's London* (Penguin, 1966), p. 208
[2] A. H. Burne, *The Battlefields of England* (Methuen, 1950), p. 100
[3] Cited by C. R. Markham, *The Yorkshire Archaeological and Topographical Journal*, Vol. 10 (1889), p. 13

IN MEMORY OF JANE FRASER

AN ATTEMPTED REPARATION

When snow like sheep lay in the fold
And winds went begging at each door
And the far hills were blue with cold
And a cold shroud lay on the moor

She kept the siege. And every day
We watched her brooding over death
Like a strong bird above its prey.
The room filled with the kettle's breath.

Damp curtains glued against the pane
Sealed time away. Her body froze
As if to freeze us all and chain
Creation to a stunned repose.

She died before the world could stir.
In March the ice unloosed the brook
And water ruffled the sun's hair.
Dead cones upon the alder shook.

1953–1967

NOTES

'In Memory of Jane Fraser' was included in my first book, *For the Unfallen*, which is now out of print. I dislike the poem very much and the publication of this amended version may be regarded as a necessary penitential exercise.

The Songbook of Sebastian Arrurruz represents the work of an apocryphal Spanish poet. Various *Cancioneros* (*Songbooks*) are referred to in bibliographies of Spanish poetry. The Arrurruz poems contain no allusion to any actual person, living or dead.